W9-BQW-099

THE IRISH IN AMERICA

THE IRISH IN AMERICA

JAMES E. JOHNSON, Ph.D.
Associate Professor of History
Bethel College

Published by
Lerner Publications Company
Minneapolis, Minnesota

...CONTENTS...

An Irish family being evicted from its home. This scene was repeated thousands of times. Millions of these miserable, poverty-stricken peasants left their native land for America.

PART I

Life on the Emerald Isle

1. *The Great Potato Famine*

More people of Irish descent live in the United States today than in Ireland. The exact number of Irish immigrants in the British colonies before the American Revolution is unknown, but it was not large. The Irish who chose to try their fortunes in America before the year 1800 were mostly independent farmers or artisans who possessed a skilled trade. The great migration of Irish people to America, however, took place in the middle of the 19th century and was connected with the potato crop. Disraeli, a famous English statesman, said that in this instance a single root changed the course of world history.

There was a potato blight in North America in 1844, and one in Europe in 1845 and subsequent years. In Ireland, it lasted for five years and proved to be a turning point in that nation's history. The story of the potato famine is one of death and disease, evictions of the people from their lands, and a mass movement by many to other countries of the earth. The only choice for some people was to stay in Ireland and starve to death or try their luck in some other place. The famine of 1845 to 1850 was so bad that nearly one-quarter of Ireland's population died of fever and disease.

2. *Life in Old Ireland*

The majority of the Irish people made their living by farming, and the life of the average Irishman was very hard. His small cottage was built of wood and sod, usually with a dirt floor. The family slept on straw, or on the ground, and their main diet was potatoes, milk, and herring. They cultivated a small garden near the house to provide them with occasional green vegetables. They usually tried to keep a pig around, which they fattened on potato peelings, and a hen or two which would provide them with eggs. The pig and the hens shared the turf house with the family since there was no other place to keep them. If they had a poor harvest, they had the choice of stealing, begging, or going hungry.

This is not to say that Ireland was normally a dreary place, for the land itself was beautiful. Ireland is often referred to as the "Emerald Isle," and with good reason. The rich green fields stood along lovely blue lakes. All of this beauty was surrounded by the ocean with its inviting views. Poets and songwriters found much in old Ireland to write about, and the people loved their land. It was true that life was often hard there if the crops failed or if an enemy invaded their shores, but the people were fiercely devoted to the green meadows and sparkling rivers.

The Irish peasant family. The huts are of sod with thatched straw roofs. Neither the father nor children have shoes.

3. *The Landlord and the Policy of Eviction*

The soil of Ireland was owned by a landed aristocracy, some of whom lived on the island, but many of whom lived in Great Britain and left the administration of their estates to managers and overseers. Though much of the soil in Ireland was better than that of England, lack of proper farming methods and money reduced the yield of the land. Whenever a man's children married they wanted to have their own plot of land, and so the size of the plots became smaller each time. There was also the fact that since all improvements reverted in the end to the owner, there was little incentive to fertilize, drain the fields, or build the fences.

By the end of the 17th century, these cottiers or landless farmers formed the great bulk of the population of Ireland. They had no rights to the soil and rented the use of enough land for a cabin and a potato patch of their own. They would often rent this land from some more fortunate farmer and would pay for it by working for the landlord as well as by sale of their pigs and eggs. Since they did not own their own land but worked for someone else, they were known as tenant farmers.

The landlord was a despised figure for the most part. He was often pictured as a cruel person who used hired agents to evict the

Poor peasants and their landlord. This picture shows under what bad conditions the simple farmers lived.

The Somerset Light Infantry assisting the police in evicting a tenant. Such evictions took place when tenants refused to pay rent to their landlords.

tenants and harass them in other ways. In general, there was little love lost between the Irish tenant farmers and the landlords. Since the Irish tenants had no long term contracts, the landlords could raise the rent at will. This process was known as "rack-renting," for the more a tenant improved his land or his livestock, the more likely he was to be hit with a rent increase. So, like a man being put to torture on a rack, the tenant was at the mercy of the landlord. At times the tenant found it advisable to give "duty gifts" to both the landlord and his overseers so that they did not raise the rent or cause trouble in some other way.

When the tenant was unable to pay the rent, the landlord often chose to drive him away. The climax came with the great famine. The potato rot, which first appeared in 1845, dragged the land and and its people through five terrible years. The number of people driven from their farms grew to 90,000 in 1849, and 100,000 in 1850.

The miserable conditions under which many of the tenant farmers lived were matched by the conditions in some of the larger cities. Dublin, with a population of 175,000 in 1830, had slums which were dirty, unpaved, unlighted, and with no water supply, sewage system, or police protection. Life in such an atmosphere was anything but easy. It is no wonder that the poor longed for a place to go where they could escape from their misery.

4. *The Decision to Go to America*

As the potato famine worsened, the lot of the Irish peasants became miserable. A Catholic parish priest told of calling on a man whose mother had been dead for two days but the man was too weak to do anything about it or prepare her for a decent burial. In one shack, the people were boiling seaweed for their meal. The starving time had arrived in Ireland and regular details of men were assigned to carry away the bodies of people who had fallen dead in the streets from disease and starvation.

The British government appropriated money to buy corn and rice for the starving poor. Great kettles were set up in the cities in which corn from the United States was boiled to provide nourishment for those who were starving. Relief ships from America, as well as packages from Irishmen living in America, brought food and clothing to the troubled land. The generous response from the United States played no small part in convincing many Irishmen that the United States was the place to live if one could find a way of getting there.

Irish emigrants leaving their home for America. This scene shows the mail coach from Cahirciveen, County Kerry, Ireland.

It was one thing to want to go to America, and another to actually find the means of going there. People of the lowest economic level are usually too poor to emigrate voluntarily. They wait until they are faced with a choice between flight and death. Such a choice now faced many Irishmen. At times a kindly landlord offered the means of escape by making free passage to America available to those of his tenants who wanted it.

Ireland, indeed, was having a time of troubles. A succession of famines, low wages, high rents, disease, unemployment, and other problems caused the British government to look upon emigration as a partial solution to the problem. It should be mentioned that some Irishmen wanted to leave because of dissatisfaction with British rule. Many detested paying tithes to a Protestant Church, since the majority of Irishmen were Roman Catholic. The Anglican Church was the state church of England, and taxes paid in Ireland were used to pay the salaries of the clergy in the Anglican Church. In the period from 1845 to 1850, however, the famine overshadowed all other causes in inducing people to leave Ireland to go to America.

The letter from America often proved to be the factor which encouraged the hesitant to pull up stakes and leave Ireland. The "letter" would usually be read to an assembled group who were eager to hear the news. It was written by one who had made the decision to go to America and now was telling of life on that side of the ocean. Often the news seemed too good to be true, but the people wanted to believe that there was a better life for them. The "letter" usually told of wages which would be impossible in Ireland, cheap lands, and freedom from military service. The size of the farms in America which the "letter" referred to was very impressive since a man who owned 30 acres was considered a large farmer in Ireland. In America, on the other hand, a 100-acre farm

The successful immigrant thinks of returning for a visit. Letters from those who had found America a land of opportunity encouraged thousands more to emigrate.

13

was common. Some wrote home of meals being served every day such as one would see only on special occasions in Ireland. One old Irish folk song, speaking of the American "letters," said:

> *They say there's land and work for all,*
> *And the sun shines always there.*

Passage to America was booked in every possible way. In the spring and early summer of 1847 the roads to the coast bristled with activity. They fled, degraded and downtrodden, and in mourning for their homes. On board ship they joined the Irish poet in sad farewell:

> *Farewell to thee, Erin mavourneen,*
> *Thy valleys I'll tread never more;*
> *This heart that now bleeds for thy sorrows,*
> *Will waste on a far distant shore.*
> *Thy green sods lie cold on my parents,*
> *A cross marks the place of their rest,—*
> *The wind that moans sadly above them,*
> *Will waft their poor child to the West.*

PART II

The Perilous Voyage

1. *Across the Wide Atlantic*

A voyage across the Atlantic Ocean in the middle 19th century could be most unpleasant. The trip to America took as long as 10 weeks on a sailing vessel if the winds were not favorable. By 1849 the time had been reduced to about 35 days from Liverpool to New York, but the conditions on board ship were terribly bad. Although the price of passage was cheap, the voyage was hard.

Passengers had to provide themselves with food. Many had nothing but oatmeal porridge sweetened with molasses, if they

The raggedy Irishman examines posters announcing sailings to New York.

could afford it. Richer ones had potatoes and salt herring. The ships seldom carried enough fresh water for drinking, to say nothing of allowing the passengers to keep themselves clean.

The Irish were crowded into close quarters below deck with not enough light or ventilation. Ship captains took as many passengers on board as they possibly could, without any thought for their comfort or safety. Disease was common and the sick were often without medical help. With inadequate toilet facilities available, the stench often became unbearable. A regular routine on some of these ships was the periodic burial services for those who had died on board.

One can imagine the eagerness which gripped the immigrants when the announcement was made that land had been sighted. Many of them expected America to be a paradise, and they looked with awe at the shores of Staten Island or the approaches to Philadelphia and Boston. Some had little bags of Irish earth which they emptied upon the ground to symbolize the wedding of Ireland and America.

2. *The Perils on Shore*

The United States of America proved to be anything but a paradise to some of the Irishmen who arrived here. Swarming about the wharves where the Irish arrived were hired men and women known as "runners." The "runners" were hired to conduct the recent arrivals to nearby hotels and boardinghouses. The new immigrant knew nothing about the value of American money, the position of boardinghouses, or how to seek employment. The "runner," therefore, who possessed an Irish brogue and wore a shamrock on his hat, seemed to be the logical person to whom the immigrant could entrust himself.

The "runners" would take the immigrants to nearby lodgings which were priced far above what they ought to be. Within a very short time the immigrant would be out of money and perhaps in

Immigrants at Castle Garden. The building was a fort during the War of 1812.

debt for his lodgings. His baggage might be confiscated until the debt was paid. Because of such difficulties, the immigrants often had to stay where they had landed and take any kind of available employment.

In 1847, a Board of Commissioners of Immigration was created in New York to supervise the inspection of ships arriving from abroad and to aid the new immigrants in every way possible. In 1855, Castle Garden, a large structure, was opened in New York as a compulsory landing place for immigrants. Those who were interested in cheating the Irish and others protested, but to no avail.

This put an end to some of the heartless exploitation of the new immigrants. Castle Garden remained New York's port of entry until Ellis Island was opened in 1892.

The Irish were specifically helped by such groups as the Hibernian Society of Philadelphia for the Relief of Emigrants, and the Irish Emigrant Society of New York. These groups reported cases where immigrants were unfairly treated, and exposed dishonest boardinghouse keepers. They published materials to be given to those Irish planning to come to the United States warning them of some of the dangers which they might encounter.

An example of the kind of cheating to which the Irish were exposed involved tickets purchased for the journey inland. These tickets provided some of the most fruitful means of fraud. The "runner," who often wore a green tie, offered to get such tickets for his new friend at advantageous prices. As a result, the Irishman found that his ticket might be good for only a portion of his journey, or it might be an utterly worthless ticket sold by a bankrupt company or one that never had existed. Unreasonably high prices were all too common. One immigrant paid $145 for a ticket that should have cost only $8.60! There was usually no way for the immigrant to protest because he had no proof of what had taken place and he could not find the party who cheated him.

It is no wonder that many of these people became discouraged and regretted their decision to leave their homeland. At times it seemed that everything and everyone was working against them. If they escaped the wretches who wanted to cheat them at their port of embarkation, they still had to face the perils at sea. If they escaped the dangers of the crossing, they had to face the friendly "runner" who wanted to relieve them of what little money they had. But dangers to the contrary, the Irishmen stayed. The next problem was to find a job. A job meant money and the realization of so many of the dreams they had of their new life in America.

PART III

Life in America

1. *Building Roads and Canals*

The life of the Irish people in Ireland did not change a great deal. Tradition is always slow to change, and the farm, the fair, the cutting of turf, the Church, and the talk of going to America remained basically the same. The uprooting process which forced the Irishman to go to America, however, opened to him other changes. For example, the 19th century Irish immigrant was not a frontiersman. He hated the lonely prairie and the great distances that were so common there. The Irishman loved having people nearby, and he did not agree with the frontier advice to move farther west when you could see the smoke of your neighbor's cabin.

The Erie Canal. Thousands of Irishmen worked as laborers in its construction.

One Irishman yearned for the simple elements of his past life as follows:

> I could then go to a fair, or a wake, or a dance . . . I could spend the winter's nights in a neighbor's house cracking jokes by the turf fire. If I had there but a sore head I could have a neighbor within every hundred yards of me that would run to see me. But here everyone can get so much land . . . that they call them neighbors that live two or three miles off.

The Irishman knew practically nothing of the farming methods in the United States, for he had never seen many of the agricultural implements in use here.

What, then, could the Irishman do for a living if he did not farm the land? Whenever the Irish settled in the interior, they usually made their presence known as laborers on internal improvement projects. Laborers were always in demand and there was usually more work to be done than hands to do it. The Irishman with his pick and shovel turned up in nearly every state of the Union, although most of them stayed in the East. They were largely responsible for the speedy completion of the network of communications which helped to make this country a great nation.

From the beginning of the last century, Irishmen were employed in road building gangs, canal projects, and in the building of railroads. In the canal building era, the contractors obtained a supply of Irish laborers by advertising in the Catholic press and in the papers of Belfast, Cork, and Dublin. Wages were high in comparison to Ireland, ranging anywhere from $.50 to $1.50 per day. The Irish helped to make New York the largest American city by the building of the Erie Canal. For a period of time, there were more Irishmen in New York City than in Dublin, and Greenwich Village was inhabited largely by poor Irish laborers.

Working conditions were severe and life was hard for the Irish. The canal diggers often stood knee-deep in water and such diseases as dysentery, cholera, and malaria were common. Accidents, cave-ins, and other injuries caused a number of deaths, as graves along the way of the canal testified. Unscrupulous contractors stirred up fights to avoid paying the men, and when it rained the workers were not paid but continued paying for board and room in the lodgings provided. The newspapers often contained reports of an Irishman drowned, or an Irishman crushed by a beam, or an Irishman suffocated in a pit, or an Irishman buried alive by the sinking of a bank. "Paddy," as the Irish laborer was often called, had to expose himself to many dangers in order to earn his daily bread.

2. *Working on the Railroad*

The road and canal eras were followed by the period of railroad construction, and the Irishman was prominent in this as well. A popular saying that there was an "Irishman buried under every

Northern Pacific workers constructing a right-of-way through the Dakota territory. Irishmen made up a large proportion of these railroad work-gangs.

tie" tells us something of the influence of the Irish. Again the newspaper accounts told of Irishmen buried under cave-ins, or Irishmen killed or maimed by blasts of powder that went off too soon.

One of the most dangerous jobs in this kind of construction was setting the blasting powder. A man would be let down with a rope over a high bank to drill holes in the rock and insert dynamite. After he lighted the fuses he would give the signal to be hauled up to safety. If the rope caught on the way up, the man perished in the explosion.

In 1839, a dollar a day was the going rate being offered to railroad workers in Pennsylvania, and this was supplemented by a daily whiskey ration of more than one pint. Many of the Irish followed the railroads west as construction progressed. They were always important as a laboring force although they were a turbulent lot, fond of whiskey, and prone to fight at the least opportunity. Some of the foremen on the Illinois Central Railroad stated their

The linking of the east and west coasts of the United States on May 10, 1869, upon completion of the first transcontinental railroad. A golden spike was driven into the last tie. The Irish were the chief nationality represented among Union Pacific laborers.

preference for German laborers because they were easier to manage than the Irish.

The Union Pacific Railroad was built by laborers representing many nationality groups, but the Irish were a very important part of the scheme. Many of the Irish veterans of the Civil War were employed by the Union Pacific Railroad because of their ability to lay down their pick and shovel and use a gun to repel Indian attacks. The Irish of the Union Pacific Railroad inspired one of America's famous folk songs entitled "Poor Paddy, He Work on the Railroad." One of the well-known stanzas is:

> *Then drill, my Paddies, drill—*
> *Drill, my heroes drill,*
> *Drill all day, no sugar in your tay,*
> *Working on the U. P. railway.*

3. *Life in the City*

The history of the Irish in America is founded on a paradox. The Irish were a rural people in Ireland and became a city people in the United States. The majority of the Irish immigrants did not move to a farm in the West, nor did they work on the internal improvement projects. They stayed in the cities of the east coast where they first arrived in America. They were penniless and had no place to go, so they settled where they were and worked.

In the middle 19th century, the majority of the carters, cabmen, and carmen in New York City were Irish. They hauled freight to the wharves, drove patrons to the theater, and performed other similar tasks. By 1860, about one-half of the foreign-born population of New York City was Irish. The influx of Irish into Boston made industrialization possible there. New England mill owners soon saw the possibilities of the Irish as a labor supply. The New England girls who had been working in the factories were independent and left as soon as they could to get married. The women insisted on decent working conditions and this increased the costs for the employers. With men available at rates lower than those paid to women, the manufacturers turned to the Irish for their labor supply.

Since the vast majority of the Irish left their ships in a port such as Boston without the slightest idea of what kind of work they would do and with only enough money to keep them for a short period of time, they ended up in two kinds of unskilled work — laborers or house servants. The Irish "serving girl" became a familiar figure in many of the households of New England. They earned from four to seven dollars a month and their room and board. Many of them had much to learn. A familiar complaint was that the Irish girls were bad at cooking meat. Few of them had much meat when they were in Ireland because they were too poor. One family said that their hired girl came downstairs backwards because she had always used a ladder in the old country! They were very welcome, however, because of their cheerful attitude, loyalty, and willingness to work for cheap wages.

We have now seen that the Irishmen stayed in America and found work to do. At the beginning, it was often work that no one else wanted to do, but time changed that. Eventually, people began to respect the cheerful attitude and willingness of the Irish immigrants, and they gained a place of high regard in American life. The busy roads, canals, and railroads over which the nation's commerce moved were proof of the contribution which the Irish were making in the building of the American nation.

Since the Irish had to live near their jobs and pay cheap rent, they moved into the slums of the eastern cities. The Irish slums of South Boston had whole families living in one room without sunlight or ventilation. Even cellars were renting for as much as $1.50 per week, and this was extremely high for that period. Such conditions encouraged overcrowding. Underground dwellings enjoyed refreshing coolness in the hot summer months and a measure of warmth in the winter. But the lack of light, air, and ordinary sanitary facilities was terrible. It is no wonder that some New Englanders were concerned with the increase in "shanty Irishmen."

The most serious danger inherent in the immigrant quarters was the complete neglect of sanitation of any kind. Privies overflowed and seeped into the streets and garbage was put outside to decay and rot. Under these circumstances, disease flourished. The water supplies were often polluted by such conditions, and the landlords did very little to remedy the conditions. One Irish slum in Boston, Broad Street, recorded one death for every 17 Irishmen in 1850. Boston had been a healthy city before the 1840's. Smallpox, for example, had been practically eliminated, but it broke out among the Irish after 1845. In 1849 a cholera epidemic spread from Philadelphia and New York to Boston and reaped a deadly harvest among the Irish there. More than 500 of the 700 fatalities were Irish.

The Irish laborers found that wages were higher in American cities than they had ever been in Ireland. But the drawbacks were many, such as the fact that they no longer had their garden patch or the pigs and chickens. Prices were very high, so that they ended up living in the slums at a subsistence level.

The question arises here as to why the Irish stayed in the slums. One answer, the economic one, has already been given. They had to live where the rent was cheap. The other factor was a simple yearning to be together with a similar group of people. Religious ties kept the Irish close to one another. Most of them were Roman Catholics and they wanted to keep their religion pure in what they considered to be a hostile environment. They would not go to the poorhouse, for example, no matter how difficult their circumstances. It was hard to get them to go to a hospital because of their fear of dying without a priest to minister to them. The Irishman's religion was his constant source of consolation amidst the many trials and sorrows which he was forced to endure.

4. *The Church and the Neighborhood*

According to Catholic sources, there were 663,000 Roman Catholics in the United States in 1840 and 1,606,000 a decade later. The church had earned its place in the affections of the Irish people. In times that were dark, priests and laymen had shared the miseries of their unhappy island. The Irish trusted their priests and found that Catholicism not only offered them salvation, but was a part of home — a place where they could recall the familiar scenes of old Ireland.

The Irish were very family conscious, and families would try desperately to stick together even if the father died. The younger members would peddle papers and do odd jobs while the older boys (12 or 13) would seek a full-time job. The mother would take in washing and do other work.

The yearning for familiar pleasures drew the immigrants together in a wide variety of activities. In Boston, the Charitable Irish Society and the Shamrock Society made St. Patrick's Day a festive occasion. The Irish were "joiners," and they loved to be a part of the militia company with its pomp and display while on parade. The thrill of being a soldier, however, could not compare to that of being a "fire laddy." Even in the largest cities, fire fighting was left to volunteers until the time of the Civil War. Each firehouse had a volunteer company and they would race the rival companies to the scene of the fire. Quite often they fought over the use of the lone fire hydrant or cistern while the building burned on.

The firemen staged elaborate parades on national holidays and other occasions. The firemen's ball was usually a gala affair, and each company would sport their own uniforms and insignia. The fire companies also had their own bands and a mascot. The Irishmen predominated on the fire company roll as well as on the police force.

Heavy drinking was all too common among the Irish. It was this common weakness, perhaps more than any other, which produced the stereotype of the red-nosed, brawling Irishman which has not yet been erased from the American mind. In 1849, Father Theobald Mathew of county Tipperary came to the United States to promote the fight against "demon rum." He convinced many thousands of

The volunteer fire company hauling its equipment "on the double." Irishmen loved the excitement of being firemen.

Irishmen to sign a "teetotaler" pledge, but he did encounter opposition. Many German and Irish Catholics advocated the continental Sunday which allowed open saloons on the Sabbath day, and so they opposed the temperance crusade of Father Mathew.

5. *The Know Nothing Movement*

Many Americans, particularly in the 1850's, believed that the continued influx of new immigrants threatened their established social structure, endangered their economic position, and spelled doom for the existing governmental system. The Irish immigrants were one of the most numerous groups to enter the country at that time, so they were the targets of persecution and opposition from the native Americans.

The opposition to immigration, and at this point, Irish immigration, was based partly on fact and partly on imagined dangers. The native Americans felt that quiet city streets were being transformed into unsightly slums by the invasion of foreigners. They could see political parties trying to obtain the votes of recent immigrants, and also an increase in intemperance, illiteracy, pauperism, and crime. Some of the people feared the threat of competition from alien laborers who were willing to work for a smaller wage than most American laborers.

Some Americans also objected to the activities of newly arrived Irish immigrants in the field of diplomacy. The Irish in America wanted their native country to be free from England, and they were anxious that the government of the United States do something to aid the Irish in obtaining this goal. Subsequently, on more than one occasion, the Irish were interested in bringing about a war between the United States and Britain with the hope that an American victory would bring freedom to Ireland. This continued Irish insistence on war with a friendly neighboring power naturally antagonized many Americans.

The forces which had been building up against the immigrants took the form of a new political party in the 1850's. This party was known as the American Party and also was often called the Know Nothing Party. The party was opposed to the continuation of a policy which allowed immigrants into the country, and it was also opposed to the Roman Catholic religion. Since the Irish were new immigrants for the most part, and since many of them were Roman Catholics, they bore the brunt of the prejudice of the Know Nothing movement.

The Know Nothing movement gained its greatest strength from 1854 to 1856. During that time the Irish immigrants, along with others, were threatened with personal violence and legislation designed to keep them in check. Their religion was suspect and their priests and nuns were accused of moral laxity and treasonable activity. The movement grew in size until they nominated their own candidate for president in the election of 1856. The party failed to make a good showing in the election and eventually declined in importance and faded into the background of the American political scene. It is important to know that the slavery issue occupied the attention of Americans, and they consequently lost interest in the Know Nothing movement. It is also well to remember that many of the Irish immigrants were shamefully treated by native Americans during this period.

PART IV

The War to Save the Union

1. *The Call to Arms*

In the pre-Civil War years there was an active movement in this country to abolish the institution of slavery. People from many walks of life such as ministers, businessmen, humanitarians, and politicians disliked slavery and wanted it done away with. They became fairly prominent in the 1830's, when the American Anti-slavery Society was formed, and continued to exercise an influence

General Philip Sheridan (1831-1888) was the son of Irish immigrants. He was considered the finest cavalry leader among Union officers.

29

up to the Civil War. Many famous Americans joined this abolition movement, and most of these individuals viewed the Civil War as a contest to free the slaves and give them the rights which other citizens enjoyed. There were many Americans, on the other hand, who opposed the abolition movement. The Irish, for the most part, did not support the movement before or during the Civil War.

The Irish were generally opposed to the abolition movement because they feared the Negro as an economic competitor. Many of them saw little difference between the factory workers of the North and the slaves of the South. The Irish were also preoccupied with their own problems. They saw so much want and need in the slums of New York City and Boston that they could not become excited about the problems of the Negro.

When Lincoln announced that the objective of the war was to save the Union, however, the Irish indicated their desire to enlist. They did not approve of the Confederacy's attempt to overthrow the government through the use of force.

Governor John A. Andrew of Massachusetts wrote the Secretary of War as follows, "Will you authorize the enlistment here . . . of Irish, Germans, and other tough men . . .? We have men of such description, eager to be employed, sufficient to make three regiments."

Irishmen who participated in the Civil War as officers for the North included Generals George Meade, Philip Sheridan, and Philip Kearney. Others were Patrick Meagher, Michael Corcoran, and John Logan. The number of Irish in the Union Army has been estimated at between 150,000 and 170,000 men. Among the distinguished Southern Irish military leaders, General Patrick Cleburne was outstanding. Though he lived in a slave state, he owned no slaves, and in 1864 advocated arming Negroes for the Confederate Army in exchange for their freedom. He served with distinction at Chickamauga and Missionary Ridge and became known as the "Stonewall Jackson of the West." He was killed at the Battle of Franklin in 1864 and Horace Greeley, editor of the *New York Tribune,* referred to his death as a "rebel disaster."

General George Meade was in command of the Union Army at Gettysburg. He prepared the defenses that Lee's forces could not penetrate.

General Philip Kearney. He lost his arm in the Mexican War and his life in the Civil War. A township was named after him in New Jersey, and the town of Kearney incorporated in 1895.

2. *The Irish Brigade*

The most famous of the Irish units in the Federal Army was the Irish Brigade, which was a part of the Army of the Potomac. Actually, the Irish Brigade consisted of the 23rd, 29th, 69th, and 88th New York Regiments, together with the 116th Pennsylvania and the 28th Massachusetts. Captain Thomas Meagher formed the 69th New York Regiment, a corps of Zouaves, and this formed the nucleus of the Irish Brigade. When the complete Irish Brigade was formed,

The Battle of Antietam, fought on September 17, 1862. The Union Army suffered 12,000 casualties, the Confederates between 8-10,000.

Captain Meagher was put in command and promoted to Brigadier General.

The Irish Brigade took part in many battles, two of the most famous being Antietam and Fredericksburg. The Irish Brigade was placed in the middle of the Federal line at Antietam. Opposite the Irish, the Confederates, under General Longstreet, had taken up a strong position in a sunken road that would be known as Bloody Lane before the day was over. The Confederate Army had built up a strong breastwork of fence rails which General William French was ordered to take. French and his men were taking a bad beating and the Irish Brigade was ordered to assist them. The Irish Brigade, 1200 strong, charged the Confederate positions and forced them to retreat. The action was costly, however, since only 500 men survived the charge and only 280 of them were able to appear on parade the next day. A soldier of the 118th Pennsylvania Volunteers, to whose rescue the Irish Brigade had come, wrote that "the gallant Irishmen moved into battle array with the precision of parade. Prominent in its place beside the national standard, the green harp of Erin was distinctly observed . . . The dead and wounded strewed the ground, thickening as the distance from the enemy lessened. Twice and again the green standard fell, but only to be promptly seized again."

The Irish Brigade moved from the action at Antietam to the Battle of Fredericksburg, where General Burnside had replaced General McClellan as the commander of the Union Army. The Confederates under General Lee held a strong position known as Marye's Heights, just beyond the town of Fredericksburg. Any attempt to try and charge the Confederate position would be suicidal, but General Burnside ordered the attack. The Irish Brigade moved up the hill as the Confederates poured a withering fire into their ranks. General Meagher had five regiments, or approximately 1500 men, to lead into battle that day. Only 263 of them survived. The Irish Brigade came to within 25 yards of the Confederate position but could get no closer because of the deadly fire from Confederate cannon and muskets. General Hancock was inspecting the Union Army the next day and asked the Irish Brigade where the rest of their company was.

"General, this is our company," they replied.

During the Peninsular Campaign in Virginia, the 69th New York Regiment was famous for its festive occasions. On May Day the men decorated the chapel with flowers and held horse and steeplechase races to break the monotony of camp life. Entry fees were collected and prizes given to the winners. They even sponsored a mule race with drummer boys as jockeys. The men decorated their huts with evergreen at Christmas and St. Patrick's Day was a time of festivity with games, dancing, and the consumption of large quantities of food and drink. Their good humor persisted even among the horrors of war.

The problem of discipline in the Union Army was by no means limited to Irish soldiers, but the latter were often a problem. The monotony of barrack life bored many Irishmen, and while in camp they proved hard to discipline. This proved to be especially true right after they received their pay.

Under the conscription law of 1863, however, the Irish had a disproportionate burden. Their resentment produced the draft riots in New York in July of that year. The bulk of Irish were laboring men who could not afford the $300 required to hire a substitute. The first drawing of names, on Saturday, July 11th, produced a list of 1200, the majority of whom were Irish. This announcement came with special impact after two years of fighting in which the Irish regiments had suffered heavy losses. There was widespread anger following Lincoln's Emancipation Proclamation the preceding autumn, for it seemed that a war begun to save the Union had turned into a war to free the Negro. The tension between the Irish and the Negroes had been growing for three months, since Negroes were used in April 1863 to break a bitter dock strike led by Irish longshoremen.

On the Monday morning following the publication of the first draft list, Irish workingmen stayed away from their jobs and began to gather in sullen crowds before the draft centers and on vacant

Confederates at Marye's Heights, the battle of Fredericksburg, December 13, 1862. The Irish charged uphill against these stone breastworks and suffered enormous casualties. The Union lost 12,650 men, the Confederates 4,200.

lots on the East side near Central Park. When the police, who themselves included great numbers of Irish, attempted under the leadership of Superintendent John Kennedy to disperse the crowds, they turned and fought. Kennedy was badly beaten. Once the rioting began, it continued for four days. The mobs went from place to place, attacking the Armory on Lexington Avenue and various private houses. The main objects of attack were Negroes. The Colored Orphan Asylum was burned; individual Negroes who were seen on the streets were beaten and several of them were hanged. It was a classic example of the poor in their misery venting their fury on the poor who were even worse off. In this case the Irish needed a scapegoat because of their resentment concerning the war and the Negro proved to be the handiest one to use.

The Irish served throughout the Civil War even though they never agreed to a war which was fought to free the slaves. They were saddened, as were most Americans, when President Abraham Lincoln was slain by John Wilkes Booth. In the subsequent years after the war, the Irish were prominently represented at the meetings of the Grand Army of the Republic, a veteran's organization.

After the Battle of Fredericksburg. This is a photograph of the Confederate position shown in the previous picture. No Union soldier broke this line, yet the Confederates suffered substantial losses.

PART V

After the Civil War

Irish energy was channeled in many directions after the Civil War. Part of it was expended in the building of the Union Pacific Railroad. The Irish had worked with the rest of American society from 1861-1865 to achieve a common goal. When the war ended, the Irish were incorporated into the expanding American society. The discrimination and prejudice which the Irish were subjected to in the period from 1840 to 1860 never again appeared in any great measure. Since the Irish had contributed their part in helping to save the Union, they were now accepted as a part of the whole.

Chinese laborers were brought in to build the Central Pacific line, and rivalry between the Irish and the Chinese was encouraged by the bosses. When the railroad was completed, the Chinese were looked upon as unfair competition and a menace. Agitation against the Chinese on the west coast was led by Dennis Kearney, an Irish-American who coined such slogans as "America for Americans" and "the Chinese must go." Pressure by Kearney's group and others against the "yellow peril" led to the passage of the Chinese Exclusion Act by the Congress in 1882. It seemed ironic that an Irishman should be involved in this kind of a movement since the Irish had been subjected to similar practices by other groups when they arrived in this country.

1. *The Fenian Movement*

The American Fenian Brotherhood was founded just prior to the Civil War. This group formed an Irish Provisional Government in exile and an Irish Liberation Army. Their aim was to free Ireland of British rule. One way they hoped to achieve their goal was by seizing Canada from the British. The Civil War temporarily diverted them from these objectives. At the conclusion of the war, the American Fenians made plans to invade Canada.

On the night of June 1, 1866, an Irish Fenian army crossed the Niagara River under the command of John O'Neill, an officer of the Civil War. O'Neill led his army of about 800 men in an attack on the Canadian Village of Fort Erie. The invaders threw up entrenchments and issued a proclamation urging the Canadians to declare their freedom from Great Britain. The Canadians gathered a force of about 2,000 men and attacked the Irish at Ridgeway, but were beaten off. The Irish were veterans of the Civil War and experienced soldiers. O'Neill realized, however, that he was greatly outnumbered and ordered his army to return to Buffalo across the Niagara River.

His whole force was then promptly captured in the name of the United States Government by forces from the *U.S.S. Michigan* on the instructions of President Andrew Johnson. General Meade, of Civil War fame, arrived with troops and seized their supplies. Thus ended a campaign which the Fenians hoped would bring revolution in Ireland and Canada, war with Great Britain, and recognition of the Irish Republic by the United States Government. Another force, which was to have invaded Canada at the same time from Vermont, fizzled out completely.

The British Government protested and claimed that the United States Government should not have allowed an invasion of Canada to be mounted from American soil by American citizens. The Irish, on the other hand, claimed that they had been betrayed by President Johnson, whom they described as a tool of the British. The Irish raised such a protest that the United States Consul in Toronto

37

hired lawyers to defend 33 Fenians who had been captured. Of these, 26 were acquitted and 7 sentenced to die, but in deference to the United States Government, these sentences were commuted to 20 years imprisonment.

2. *The Molly Maguires*

The Irish gravitated to the coal fields in Pennsylvania. Working conditions in the mines caused them to form a secret organization known as the Molly Maguires. Nobody knew the identity of the Molly Maguires, other than the Mollies themselves. Nobody knew when they met or who was to be their next victim or who was their

An Irish work-gang in the early 1890's.

leader. A miner might wonder if the man working next to him was a member of the organization but he knew better than to ask.

Among the miners there was a conspiracy of silence concerning the Molly Maguires. This was due to fear on the part of some, and agreement among the rest. The men whom the Mollies picked as their victims were often cruel and callous bosses who exploited the miners on every opportunity.

Conditions in the coal mines caused the Molly Maguires to grow. Miners toiled for long hours under very dangerous conditions. If a miner was paid by weight, he was frequently cheated. A checkman estimated the amount of coal each miner produced and his word was law. If the miner was paid by the car load, the size of the car might be increased while the pay remained the same. Miners were often forced to live in company homes and buy their groceries at a company store. A company store could be operated to the disadvantage of the miner, as the following list illustrates:

Coal mined, 40 tons at 60 cents = $24.00

Supplies	$ 7.50
Blacksmith	.25
Drill repair	.25
Rent	6.00
Groceries	10.00
	$24.00

This miner was in no better condition than a slave in the South before the Civil War. He never could get ahead under such a bookkeeping system. In fact, the slave would probably never work at any job as dangerous as coal mining.

Children were often employed in the breaker room. Here the coal flowed in an unending stream as boys as young as six years of age separated the slate from the coal and broke up the larger lumps. Old men with hunched shoulders and bent spines, a characteristic after years in the mine, worked side by side with them. The boys could see their future laid out before them. From the breaker they would go to the mines and work as long as their health held up, and then back to the breakers again. The Molly Maguires became the means by which the miners could register their protest regarding such working conditions.

The mine operators decided to strike back, and led by Franklin B. Gowen, President of the Philadelphia and Reading Railroad Company, they turned to the Pinkerton Detective Agency in Chicago for help. Pinkerton chose a young Irishman, named James McParland, for the task and sent him alone to the coal fields to see what he could do.

James McParland was born in County Armagh, Ireland, and came to the United States in 1867. He had dark hair, blue eyes, could sing and dance, and was a handy man with his fists. He changed his name to McKenna and went to Pottsville, Pennsylvania to begin work. His instructions were to uncover details of the crimes being planned by the Mollies with the object of making arrests when the evidence warranted this. He never completely succeeded in carrying out his mission, but he uncovered evidence regarding murders and other crimes committed by the Mollies. This evidence was crucial in several later cases leading to the conviction of some members of the Molly Maguires. McParland was completely accepted by the Irish mining community until a railroad conductor stumbled on the fact that he was a detective in the pay of the management.

Pinkerton Detective
James McParland.

He left town and took much of his evidence with him. Arrests were made and trials held, and 19 men were eventually hanged for crimes they had committed. McParland went back to Chicago and continued to work for the Pinkerton Agency. The Molly Maguires lost much of their influence and never again were an important part of the Irish coal mining community in Pennsylvania. The unfortunate legacy of the Molly Maguires was that many people in America associated all labor union movements with the violent tactics of the Mollies.

3. *The Irish and the Modern Trade Unions*

The laborer in America has made great progress since the days of the Molly Maguire movement in Pennsylvania. The Irish, of course, have shared in this progress and have participated in the trade union movement which has helped to bring it about.

Perhaps the best example of an Irishman who has risen through the ranks is George Meany. He began as a plumber. In 1953, Meany became President of the American Federation of Labor, the highest post in the trade union movement. Another Irish labor leader is Albert J. Fitzgerald, the president of the United Electrical Radio and Machine Workers of America.

George Meany, president of the American Federation of Labor-Congress of Industrial Organizations.

41

Michael J. Quill, president of the Transport Workers Union and leader of the New York subway strike in 1966, was a well-known Irish labor official. John Mitchell, president of the United Mine Workers of America in 1898, was an Irishman who became involved in a serious strike with the mine owners in 1902. President Theodore Roosevelt had to intervene in order to bring that strike to an end. Peter McGuire, the Irish founder of the Brotherhood of Carpenters and Joiners, was the man who proposed a yearly national holiday called "Labor Day." Congress liked the idea and made it official, and most school children know that they usually return to school soon after Labor Day in September.

The Irish did get something for all of the back-breaking work they did on the nation's roads, canals, and railroads. You will find Irish names connected with many of the big city construction companies in America. Some of the more common of these names are: McShane, Tully, Farley, Foley, Kelly, Walsh, and Driscoll.

PART VI

Famous Americans of Irish Ancestry

The American Irishman was almost always costumed on the stage in ragged, dirty clothes. His manner was impudent and pugnacious; he was usually an eloquent braggard, and a master with the shillelagh. A conscious effort was made at the turn of the century to get rid of some of these stereotypes. The "Shanty Irish" and the "Fighting Irish" were played down as much as possible. Stereotypes remained, however, in spite of these efforts. The Hearst papers still carry a comic strip entitled "Maggie and Jiggs." Maggie is pictured as a social climber who wants to go to the opera and meet the right people. Jiggs, on the other hand, wants to take his shoes off at home and enjoy his corned beef and cabbage. Better yet, he likes to enjoy an occasional glass with the boys down at Dinty Moore's.

1. *Irish Literary Figures*

Irish writers are almost too numerous to mention. Among them was Peter Finley Dunne, one of America's great satirists. Dunne was born in Chicago in 1867, and created a legendary character, Mr. Dooley, a saloon keeper, and his patron, Hennessey. Hennessey proved to be a patient listener as Mr. Dooley commented on the affairs of the day. Dunne's humor and insights were widely enjoyed. He is recognized today as a political commentator who voiced the sentiments of the Irish community.

America's greatest playwright, and the second American to win the Nobel prize for literature, was Eugene O'Neill, whose father, James, came to America as a child after the great potato famine. James became a Shakespearean actor and also played the lead in *The Count of Monte Cristo.* His son was baptized Eugene Gladstone O'Neill because of the father's admiration for the British Prime Minister who tried to help Ireland.

Eugene O'Neill received a Catholic parochial school education, but, as a young man, he broke away from the Catholic Church. He spent a year at Princeton, sailed on merchant vessels, and explored for gold in Central America. In 1912 he was reunited with his family in New London, Connecticut. He discovered that he had tuberculosis and entered a sanitorium for treatment. It was there he decided that he would like to write plays. Eight years later he received a Pulitzer Prize.

Eugene O'Neill. He received the Nobel prize for literature in 1936. The Pulitzer prize for drama was awarded to him four times: in 1920, 1922, 1928, and 1957.

O'Neill was proud of his Irish heritage. He considered it as a great compliment when Sean O'Casey said, "You write like an Irishman, not like an American." He was proud of the fact that his family name in Gaelic meant champion, and he liked to think of himself as being descended from Shane the Proud. Shane was an Irish warrior who became involved in a swimming race with another warrior. Shane realized that he was not going to win so he took out his dagger and cut off his hand. He then flung the hand to the far shore and won the fair lady, since the stipulation was that the man whose hand first touched the shore would get the prize. Some of O'Neill's well-known works are: *The Hairy Ape, Desire Under the Elms, The Iceman Cometh,* and *Long Day's Journey Into Night.*

F. Scott Fitzgerald, the famous novelist, was named after the author of our national anthem. He is known for many works, among which are *This Side of Paradise, The Great Gatsby,* and *Tender is the Night.* Another Irishman, John O'Hara, wrote *Butterfield 8,* the musical comedy *Pal Joey* and other books. James T. Farrell has written numerous volumes, primarily dealing with the life of the Irish in Chicago.

F. SCOTT FITZGERALD   JOHN O'HARA   JAMES T. FARRELL

2. Music

The Irish, it has been said, are a people who have "music in their souls." One could not gather a group of Irishmen together for long without music filling the air. The words and music of the Irish songs followed a common pattern. They told about what the immigrant had left behind and what he missed and longed for. Usually they were simple things — the song of a thrush at twilight, the familiar woods, the cattle grazing on emerald-green meadows, and the beautiful distant mountains. Some of the songs would tell of the sea, or a saintly old mother, or a lover over the hill.

Songs of love and longing outnumber all other categories. Some Irish love songs are known to millions, such as *Sweet Rosie O'Grady* or *I'll Take You Home Again Kathleen*. Some of these, which have become a part of America's treasure-house of song, were written by composers who were not Irish and had never seen Ireland.

John McCormack, a great Irish tenor, for years featured a song of reverence for motherhood, *Mother Machree*. This song was written by Earnest R. Ball, a Cleveland composer who also wrote *When Irish Eyes Are Smiling*. Chauncy Olcott made *My Wild Irish Rose* an American classic in 1899. Olcott was American born, but of Irish ancestry, and he built up a loyal Irish following with his many plays and songs.

Patrick Gilmore, another Irishman with a musical flair, recruited and trained army bands during the Civil War. He was fond of giant festivals such as the World Peace Jubilee held in 1872. This gala affair had mammoth bands, the firing of cannon, the ringing of church bells, and 50 firemen beating out the *Anvil Chorus* on 50 anvils. Gilmore wrote the words for *When Johnny Comes Marching Home*.

George M. Cohan epitomized the genial, witty, sentimental, and lighthearted Irishman. He was born in 1878, and his career of 50 years reached from the melodrama of the Gilded Age to the realistic plays of the 1930's. Cohan was a public personality and a songwriter and he expressed the passionate patriotism of the

George M. Cohan. He wrote *I'm A Yankee Doodle Dandy,*
and many songs of World War I.

second generation Irishman. It is no accident that he wrote the
most popular patriotic song of World War I, *Over There.*

One of the more recent Irish musicians, born in Dublin, was
Victor Herbert. He began his career in the United States as a
cellist with symphony orchestras and finally became a conductor.
He wrote the scores for several of Ziegfeld's Follies as well as
many light operas. Herbert was President of the American-Irish
Society and the Friendly Sons of St. Patrick.

Victor Herbert. He composed numerous light operas, including *Babes
in Toyland, Naughty Marietta,* and *The Red Mill.*

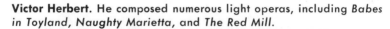

BING CROSBY   JACKIE GLEASON   GRACE KELLY

The entertainment world contains numerous prominent individuals of Irish ancestry. Bing Crosby started as a singer with a dance band in the 1930's, and rose to become one of America's best known performers. He has starred in movies and in television for many years. Crosby made the whole nation aware of the song *I'm Dreaming of a White Christmas* a few years ago and one of his most loved songs has been *An Irish Lullaby*. Others in the entertainment world have been movie stars Maureen O'Hara, Peter Lind Hayes, Morton Downey, Jackie Gleason, Arthur Godfrey, Pat O'Brien, Barbara Stanwyck, Helen Hayes, Fred Allen, and James Cagney. Grace Kelly of Philadelphia was known for her career as a

Helen Hayes. She is depicted in her role of Harriet Beecher Stowe.

Fred Allen, shown together with a co-star of his, Ginger Rogers.

Ed Sullivan. He is known to millions because of his weekly television broadcasts.

movie star before she married Prince Rainier of Monaco. The Ed Sullivan variety show is familiar to millions of Americans.

3. Sports

One way for a poor immigrant to rise in the world was by the use of his fists. The Irish contributed many fighters who rose to be champions. Perhaps the best known of all time is John L. Sullivan. He stood 5' 10" and weighed 190 lbs. His power came from his broad shoulders, long arms, and strong hands. In 1877 he attended a boxing exhibition at the Dudley Street Opera House in Boston. Tom Scannel, a well-known local fighter, challenged all comers, and Sullivan went into the ring and finished him off quickly.

Sullivan then came under the management of William Muldoon, who had a genius for publicity. He took Sullivan on a nation-wide tour and offered $50 to anyone who could stay in the ring with him for four rounds. Sullivan once fought a blacksmith who was over

John L. Sullivan, heavyweight boxing champion from 1882-1892.

49

seven feet tall. He merely hammered at the man's stomach until he had to bend over and then the "Boston strong boy" finished him off. He finally got a match with Paddy Ryan, the champion. The fight was conducted under the London Prize Ring rules, which meant that bare knuckles and gouging were permitted. The fight lasted for nine rounds after which Sullivan was the new champion.

Sullivan actually preferred the Marquis of Queensbury Rules and established them in this country. Under these rules, each man was to wear five-ounce boxing gloves and gouging was prohibited. Sullivan quickly became the idol of Boston and the nation's hero. In 1887, the city of Boston presented him with a diamond and gold belt valued at $10,000. By 1892, Sullivan had earned more than half-a-million dollars and had spent all of it. On September 7, 1892, Sullivan was defeated by another Irishman, "Gentleman Jim" Corbett. When John L. Sullivan died on February 6, 1918, thousands of people lined the streets of Boston to pay their last respects to the champion.

Jack Dempsey, heavyweight boxing champion from 1919-1926.

The prize fight in the United States proved to be the ladder of success for many Irish boys. Among them have been: Jake Kilrain, Mike McTigue, Tom Sharkey, Packy McFarland, Tommy Gibbons, Billy Conn, Jack Dempsey, Gene Tunney, Tommy Burns, Jack Sharkey, and Jim Braddock.

The Irish also participated in the great American game of baseball. John Joseph ("Muggsy") McGraw, of Truxton, New Jersey, played infield for the Baltimore Orioles. After a short stay with the Orioles, he began managing the New York Giants in 1902 when he was only 29 years of age. His teams won 10 National League pennants. Other Irish big league managers were: Pat Moran, Joe McCarthy (manager of the New York Yankees when they won several pennants), and Joe Cronin. One of the most famous was Cornelius McGillicuddy (Connie Mack), who was the grand old man of baseball until his death on February 8, 1956.

Charles A. Comiskey, who played third base for Milwaukee at the age of 17, enjoyed a long career as a player. After that he helped to organize the American League and was the President of the Chicago White Sox from its beginning in 1900 until his death in 1931. In baseball's Hall of Fame at Cooperstown, New York, the Irish are represented by Joe Cronin, Connie Mack, Joseph (Iron Man) McGinnty, Jim O'Rourke, King Kelly, George (Mickey) Cochrane, one of the great catchers of all time, and Hugh Duffy, an outfielder who batted .438 in 1894.

CONNIE MACK   **JOSEPH EDWARD CRONIN**   **"MICKEY" COCHRANE**

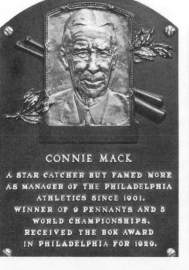

CONNIE MACK

A STAR CATCHER BUT FAMED MORE AS MANAGER OF THE PHILADELPHIA ATHLETICS SINCE 1901. WINNER OF 9 PENNANTS AND 5 WORLD CHAMPIONSHIPS. RECEIVED THE BOK AWARD IN PHILADELPHIA FOR 1929.

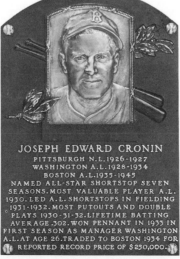

JOSEPH EDWARD CRONIN
PITTSBURGH N.L.1926-1927
WASHINGTON A.L.1928-1934
BOSTON A.L.1935-1945
NAMED ALL-STAR SHORTSTOP SEVEN SEASONS. MOST VALUABLE PLAYER A.L. 1930. LED A.L. SHORTSTOPS IN FIELDING 1931-1932. MOST PUTOUTS AND DOUBLE PLAYS 1930-31-32. LIFETIME BATTING AVERAGE .302. WON PENNANT IN 1933 IN FIRST SEASON AS MANAGER WASHINGTON A.L. AT AGE 26. TRADED TO BOSTON 1934 FOR REPORTED RECORD PRICE OF $250,000.

GORDON "MICKEY" COCHRANE
PHILADELPHIA A.L.1925-1933
DETROIT A.L.1934-1937
FIERY CATCHER COMPILED A NOTABLE RECORD BOTH AS A PLAYER AND MANAGER. THE SPARK OF THE ATHLETICS' CHAMPIONSHIP TEAMS OF 1929-30-31, HAD AN AVERAGE BATTING MARK OF .346 FOR THOSE THREE YEARS. LED DETROIT TO TWO LEAGUE CHAMPIONSHIPS AND A WORLD SERIES TITLE IN 1935.

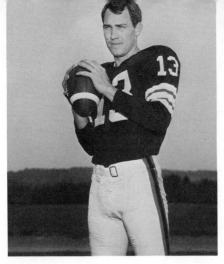

Frank Ryan, star quarterback for the Cleveland Browns.

Ben Hogan, one of the greatest golfers of all time.

In football, of course, the players at Notre Dame University have been known for years as the "Fighting Irish." There are several Irish players involved in the ranks of professional football today.

Ben Hogan, one of America's all-time golf greats, won the United States Open Championship four times, in 1948, 1950, 1951 and 1953.

4. *Service in the Church*

Many Irishmen naturally chose the church as their place of service in life. Three of them were Cardinal James Gibbons, Archbishop John Ireland, and Monsignor John A. Ryan. Archbishop Ireland came from county Kilkenny and went with his family by covered wagon to Minnesota in the 1850's. His father was a carpenter and a local Democratic politician. Father Ireland became a priest in St. Paul, Minnesota in 1861. During the Civil War he served in the Union Army as a Chaplain. He was an ardent reformer who fought municipal corruption, a Republican, and a friend of President Theodore Roosevelt. His liberal views about the school question and the role of the church in civic affairs brought him into conflict with many of his fellow bishops. He never received appoint-

ARCHBISHOP JOHN IRELAND

ment as a cardinal although his friend President Roosevelt wanted it for him.

John Augustine Ryan was born in 1869 about 20 miles south of St. Paul, Minnesota, one of 11 children of an Irish immigrant couple. He went to public school and the Christian Brother's school in St. Paul, and also spent some of his afternoons in the State Legislature listening to his hero, Ignatius Donnelly. Mr. Donnelly was one of the great speakers of the Populist Party. Ryan's preparation for the priesthood was obtained at the new St. Paul Seminary. He became one of the leading spokesmen for the liberal Catholic social philosophy.

Cardinal James Gibbons was born in Baltimore in 1834. He was taken back to Ireland at the age of three, where his father died of a fever during the famine of 1847. Returning to the United States in 1849, he entered a seminary in New Orleans and embarked upon his studies for the priesthood. He was a recipient of a cardinal's red hat in 1887, being the second American to be so honored up to that time.

CARDINAL JAMES GIBBONS

Cardinal Gibbons found his greatness as a diplomat. He possessed a wide tolerance and flexibility toward others, and realized very sensibly that the Irish were not the only national group included in the Roman Catholic Church. He liked to smoke cigars, and when visiting a friend of his in Ireland who disliked tobacco, he confined his smoking to his room. When a visitor inquired of the pastor if the cardinal was in, the priest replied, "Yes, don't you smell him?"

He was a good friend of Archbishop John Ireland of St. Paul, but he gave no hint of his voting attitudes, while Archbishop Ireland was outspoken in his bias for the Republican Party. When Archbishop Ireland heard that Cardinal Gibbons had been invited to deliver a prayer at the opening of the Democratic National Convention, he said to him, "Be on your guard while invoking blessings upon the Democratic National Convention. Pray hard for the country, not so much for the party."

Cardinal Gibbons had suffered from ill health as a young priest. In fact, it was feared that he had tuberculosis. He died in 1921 at the age of 87. When asked for the prescription to a long life, just prior to his death, he said, "Acquire an incurable ailment in your youth."

5. Architecture

Louis Henry Sullivan, the son of a wandering Irish musician, was America's first great modern architect. He was a man ahead of his times, who designed many buildings which his contemporaries disliked, but which since that time have often been regarded as models of grace and beauty. He completed the Security Bank and Trust Company of Owatonna, Minnesota in 1908. This building was allowed to fall into a state of disrepair for many years, but has been completely restored in more recent times. A plaque, located in the bank lobby, reads as follows:

LOUIS H. SULLIVAN

A Monument

To His Architectural Vision

And Leadership

His other masterpieces include the Auditorium Building in Chicago, which now houses Roosevelt University.

Louis H. Sullivan, *(left)* famed pioneer architect of the skyscraper.

The Auditorium Building, *(below)* Chicago, Illinois, designed by Louis Sullivan. It once housed the Chicago Opera Company. Today it is the home of Roosevelt University.

Lt. Col. William J. Donovan, in World War I. Notice the ribbons. One represents the Distinguished Service Cross, for bravery at Chateau Thierry. The other is the Croix de Guerre, France's highest honor.

Colin P. Kelly, World War II hero. Japan attacked Pearl Harbor on December 7, 1941. On December 10, 1941, Kelly lost his life in an attack for which he received our nation's highest military award.

Admiral William D. Leahy *(far left)* participates in the ceremony where President Truman proclaims the surrender of Japan. A prominent Irish political figure, James Byrnes, then Secretary of State, sits next to Leahy.

6. *The Military*

The Irish have been involved in the military establishment of this country from its earliest days. George Washington had a general serving under him named Sullivan who carried out several successful campaigns. The part which the Irish played in the Civil War has been told elsewhere and need not be repeated.

The 69th New York Regiment (part of the Civil War Irish Brigade) stayed together as a unit. They were one of the first to be sent to France when America entered World War I. For a period of about 180 days they were in direct contact with the enemy, and they changed their headquarters some 83 times. The outfit went overseas with 3500 men, and it suffered exactly 3501 casualties; 644 killed and 2857 wounded. The leader of the "Fighting 69th" was General William J. (Wild Bill) Donovan. He also served as chief of the Office of Strategic Services in World War II.

Colin P. Kelly, a 26-year-old West Pointer, became one of the first war heroes in World War II. On December 10, 1941, he took off in a Flying Fortress bomber from Clark Field in the Philippine Islands. Since the Japanese had attacked the United States Naval Base at Pearl Harbor three days previously, his mission was to destroy a Japanese aircraft carrier operating north of the island of Luzon. They finally spotted some Japanese ships and scored two hits on the Japanese battleship *Haruna*. They headed for home but were intercepted by Japanese fighter planes. Kelly ordered the crew out as the ship began to burn but before he could get away the plane exploded. General MacArthur posthumously awarded Kelly the Distinguished Service Cross.

Other Irishmen who have served in the military forces have been Admiral of the Fleet William D. Leahy and Major General Patrick J. Hurley. General Hurley was Secretary of War under President Hoover and Ambassador to China in the 1940's.

DR. TOM DOOLEY

One of the most inspiring stories of modern times is that of Dr. Tom Dooley, who died of cancer at the age of 34. Upon graduation from the School of Medicine at St. Louis University, he entered the Navy. His ship was assigned to participate in the evacuation of thousands of Vietnamese who were fleeing from the Communist regime in the North. He was mustered out of the service but could not forget the land he had left. He subsequently went to Laos with his old staff of Navy corpsmen to help him and with supplies which had been contributed. He did not spare himself and helped to found an organization known as MEDICO. Before his death in 1961, he made possible the establishment of 18 hospitals and clinics in 12 countries.

7. *Business*

Many Irishmen have succeeded in the field of business. One example would be Emmet J. McCormack, the co-founder and chairman of the Moore-McCormack Lines. He was born in Brooklyn, the son of Irish immigrants, and he became the head of one of the largest American-flag steamship lines in the world. As a youth he sold rope, coal, and other marine supplies in the waterfront area of New York City. By the time he was 25, he had saved enough to open his own concern, the Commercial Coal Company. Then he salvaged an old ferryboat sunken off the New Jersey shoreline in exchange for its use for six years. He joined with a friend, Albert Moore, in 1913 and formed the Moore and McCormack Company, Inc. In another 25 years they had added 24 other companies and formed the Moore-McCormack Lines, Inc., which today has assets exceeding 130 million dollars.

A similar business run by Irishmen is the Grace Line, Inc. William R. Grace, the founder of the Grace Line, got his first job in America as a singing waiter. He later became a longshoreman and finally launched the company which bears his name.

There have been other Irishmen of note as well. John MacDonald, son of an Irish immigrant from Tipperary, was so important in the building of the New York subways that when he died in 1911, all power on the subways was shut off for two minutes as a tribute. The builder of one of New York's first skyscrapers, Daniel Crimmins, was the son of Irish immigrants. He was responsible for the construction of some 400 buildings in New York City, the elevated railroads, and the paving of the whole of New York's Broadway. John Robert Gregg, who became weary of note taking in his studies, perfected a simple system of shorthand. John Wolfe Ambrose dredged a deep-water channel into New York harbor, and the beacon that guides vessels into anchorage, Ambrose Light, is named for him. John F. O'Rourke planned and built part of New York's subway system. Marcus Daly helped establish the Anaconda mining empire, and John Mackay, Dublin born, discovered the famous Comstock lode in Nevada.

PART VII

The Irish in Politics

Politics was an attractive career for the Irish in America. It was one of the few professions where it was an asset, rather than a drawback, to be an immigrant. A minimum amount of education was sufficient to prepare for it and the rewards came to the successful in a relatively short time. The Irish became active in the building of political machines in the cities of the North and Midwest. Family ties, neighborhood loyalties, and the fact that recently arrived immigrants were willing to give their vote to one of their own kind, provided the foundation of power.

1. *The Political Machine*

The political machine existed primarily because of the needs it was able to fulfill. The immigrant family seeking work, the widowed mother without funds, the truant boy in trouble with the police, and the injured workman, all needed someone to help them. In exchange, they were willing to give their votes. Since the Irish were the most numerous group in many cities, they took over and provided almost a parallel system of government. Charm, boldness, and a fluent tongue, traits common to many Irishmen, were the necessary criteria for a career in politics.

One of the most famous of the large city political organizations was the Tammany Club in New York City. It was named in honor of a famous 17th century chief of the Delaware Indians. The 12 leaders were known as sachems, or chiefs, and the group was intended primarily as a fraternal and charitable order.

Tammany Hall was the Democratic party in New York City and the Irish were attracted to both because they felt that the interests of the lower classes would be protected there. Tammany Hall learned quickly that favors given to poor Irish immigrants paid dividends at the polls. They provided legal aid to immigrants in trouble, bailed out petty offenders, and found jobs or the means to get an education for the brighter youngsters.

The political boss usually was the overseer of this activity. Some bosses thought of themselves as modern Robin Hoods who robbed the rich to help feed the poor. They would send flowers to funerals, coal to those who needed warmth, and dinners for the poor on Christmas day. One of the worst examples of a political boss was William Marcy Tweed, who ruled over Tammany Hall for a period after the Civil War. Tweed was a great bulk of a man, standing just under six feet and weighing about 300 lbs. Tweed and Tammany Hall ran the city of New York even though they knew practically nothing about the machinery of government. Actually, they spent most of their time looting the city treasury. In six years time, they drained the city of nearly six million dollars. The mayor of New York, Oakey Hall, worked with Boss Tweed and his gang. One New York newspaper said that the city was being governed by Oakey Hall, Tammany Hall, and alcohol! When Boss Tweed and his gang were finally exposed and driven from positions of responsibility, they still were respected by the poorer classes of the city to whom they had extended so much help. Tweed was not an Irishman, but his successors, Richard Croker and Charles F. Murphy, were both Irish.

The power of the Irish vote was clearly demonstrated in the election of 1884. James G. Blaine was the Republican candidate and Grover Cleveland was running on the Democratic ticket. Blaine seemed to be making inroads among the Democratic party voters and the party leaders were quite worried. An event occurred, however, which changed the whole course of the election.

The Rev. Dr. Samuel D. Burchard, a Presbyterian clergyman, referred to the Democratic party as the party of "Rum, Romanism, and Rebellion" and the reaction was reflected at the polls. The Irish flocked to Grover Cleveland's support and he won the election.

Woodrow Wilson, President of the United States during World War I, had some problems with the Irish. As early as May 1914, at the dedication of a monument to John Barry, the Irish-American Naval Commander, Wilson had made some sharp remarks about the patriotism of the foreign-born. He had referred to Barry as an Irishman whose "heart crossed the Atlantic with him," and criticized Americans who "need hyphens in their names because only part of them has come over." The Irish resented these remarks. President Wilson was very sympathetic to the side of Great Britain in her war with Germany, but the Irish hated the British for refusing to give Ireland her freedom. Jeremiah O'Leary, the President of the pro-German American Truth Society, sent Wilson an insulting telegram accusing him of becoming a dictator and bowing his knee to England. Wilson retorted that he wanted no support from the disloyal. Wilson also had difficulties with the Irish-American community because he did not push the cause of Irish independence at the Peace Conference in Paris as hard as they felt that he should. This is not to imply that the Irish-Americans lacked patriotism. On the contrary, the 69th division of Civil War fame went to France during the First World War and became known for its valor as the "Fighting 69th."

2. Municipal Politics

James Michael Curley was born in Boston on the 20th day of November, 1874. He ran for his first office in 1899 and was alternately mayor of Boston and governor of Massachusetts from 1921 until 1949. He had a large and fashionable home in Boston with an exterior that was distinguished by a shamrock carved on each of its shutters. His adeptness in finding a political issue can be shown by the account given in his autobiography of what he did for the scrubwomen of Boston: "My mother was obliged to work . . . as a scrubwoman toiling nights in office buildings downtown. I thought of her one night while leaving City Hall during my first term as mayor. I told the scrubwomen cleaning the corridors to get up: 'The only time a woman should go down on her knees is when she is praying to Almighty God,' I said. Next morning I ordered long-handled mops and issued an order that scrubwomen were never again to get down on their knees in City Hall."

Edwin O'Connor wrote a novel entitled *The Last Hurrah* which was modeled on Curley's life. It shows the Irish politician at work among his constituents, attending their wakes, weddings, and graduations, and making as many friends as he possibly can. The more friends that he makes, the more votes he can count on in the next election.

The Chicago mayor, Richard J. Daley, is a short, ruddy-faced, wide-shouldered Irish Catholic. He is probably the most powerful political boss in Illinois' history. Mayor Daley knows the game of politics as few people do. He grew up in the "Back of the Stock-yards" neighborhood of Chicago, and had to fight for everything

RICHARD J. DALEY

he obtained. After becoming a precinct captain at age 21, he successively became State Representative, State Senator, Secretary to four county treasurers, county comptroller, and state director of finance.

Mayor Daley begins his day around 7:00 a.m. by having breakfast with his family and occasionally attending mass at the local parish church. He jots down notes, while being driven to his office, of things to be done for that day. He has an almost encyclopedic memory and works hard at his job. He is devoted to his family and was publicized as an All-American father of seven children, one of whom is a nun. If he has no banquets or other civic functions to attend, he circulates among the voters. One of his associates claims that he has his name in more "wake books" than any other person in Chicago's history.

The Chicago Mayor's office is one of the most powerful political positions in the country. As Cook County Democratic Chairman, Mayor Daley says much about who will be governor of the state of Illinois. He controls an empire of over 10,000 patronage jobs and a variety of other political favors. His administration has been instrumental in promoting the development of Chicago, enlarging the O'Hare airport, constructing more expressways, and recruiting new industry.

3. *National Politics*

Another Irish politician who rose through the ranks was Al Smith of New York City. His father was a teamster who worked hard and spent long hours driving his team of horses through the streets of New York. The father died when Al was 13 years old and the boy quit school two years later to take a job. He often expressed his regret at being deprived of an education. In 1903 the Democratic organization sent Smith to the State Assembly where he worked up to the position of Speaker and served on several committees. He was elected governor of the state in 1918 and was re-elected in 1922.

Alfred Emanuel (Al) Smith, twice governor of New York, and the first Irishman to run for President of the United States.

In 1928 Al Smith became the Democratic Party nominee for the office of President of the United States. His opponent was Herbert Hoover. Few elections in American history have been characterized by as much mud-slinging as that of 1928. Smith was an Irishman, a Roman Catholic, and was in favor of the repeal of the Prohibition Amendment. He was slandered on all three counts. As an Irishman from the sidewalks of New York, he was looked down upon by some other groups of Americans. As a Roman Catholic, his religion counted against him since no Catholic had yet ever been elected to the office of President. As a "wet" in favor of the repeal of prohibition, he came under attack from the "drys." Smith polled 15.5 million votes and one-third of them came from the industrial states of Connecticut, Illinois, Massachusetts, New Jersey, and New York. Since the Irish were heavily concentrated in the industrial cities, it would be fair to assume that Smith captured most of the Irish vote. It would be unfair, however, to say that Smith was defeated merely because he was Irish, Catholic, and "wet." The Republican Party had a strong candidate in Herbert Hoover and the prosperity which the country was enjoying was in their favor. Many people did not want to make any change while things were going so well. Will Rogers, a famous Hollywood personality, touched a sore spot when he told Smith that he "had no issue." Most people were willing to stay with the Republican Party and prosperity unless Smith and the Democrats had something better to offer.

John W. McCormack, Speaker of the House of Representatives, is from the 9th Congressional District of Massachusetts.

When Franklin D. Roosevelt assumed the office of President of the United States in 1933, he appointed several Irishmen to posts in his administration. Among them were Thomas Corcoran, John McCormack, James Farley, Edward Flynn, Thomas Walsh and Joseph Kennedy.

Thomas Corcoran, known as "Tommy the Cork," was born in Pawtucket, Rhode Island on December 29, 1900. He was valedictorian at Brown University and a graduate of Harvard Law School. He went to work for the Reconstruction Finance Corporation in 1932 and became a member of the famous "Brain Trust," a group of high level advisors to President Roosevelt during the days of the "New Deal."

John W. McCormack, Congressman from Massachusetts, gave the New Deal strong support in the 1930's and had the opportunity of introducing the Lend Lease Bill in the House of Representatives. He became Speaker of the House of Representatives in 1961.

James A. Farley, former Postmaster General and now chairman of the Board of the Coca-Cola Export Corporation. He managed the successful presidential campaigns of Franklin D. Roosevelt in 1932 and 1936.

James Aloysius Farley grew up in the town of Grassy Point, some 35 miles north of New York City. He worked up through minor political offices and was appointed to the State Boxing Commission by Governor Al Smith. When he became chairman of the Boxing Commission, he cultivated many friends by passing out thousands of dollars worth of tickets. In 1928 he ran Franklin Roosevelt's campaign for governor while occupying the post of Secretary of the Democratic State Committee. By 1930 he was state chairman of the Democratic Committee and he revealed his remarkable ability to remember names while touring the country. It was said that he could remember the first names of 10,000 people. It is significant that all the personal notes he wrote to individuals were in green ink! President Roosevelt appointed him to the office of Postmaster General in 1933. He proved to be a key man in the Roosevelt administration where he dispensed patronage with a view towards getting more votes. Farley broke with Roosevelt in 1940 when the latter decided to run for a third term in office.

Mr. Farley is presently the Chairman of the Board of the Coca-Cola Export Corporation. In 1963 he traveled a total of 53,000 miles, attending 98 dinners and 78 business luncheons. He also visited the home of his Irish ancestors near Ceanannus Mor, from whence his grandparents left for the United States in 1840. He was the late President Kennedy's representative at the Requiem Mass for Pope John in Rome. He is a devout Catholic and is very proud of his Irish ancestry. He holds 31 honorary degrees, citations and decorations, and is the author of two books, *Behind the Ballots* and *Jim Farley's Story.*

An Irishman who became very well-known in the post-World War II period was Senator Joseph McCarthy of Wisconsin. McCarthy was born near Appleton, Wisconsin in 1908. He attended school in that area and then Marquette University. He was admitted to the bar, dabbled in politics and joined the Marine Corps in 1942. Commissioned a 2nd Lieutenant, he had a routine ground assignment in which he recorded information given by pilots who had flown missions. In 1946 he upset Robert M. La Follette Jr. in the

Republican senatorial primary, and then went on to win election as Wisconsin's junior senator. In 1950 McCarthy began to investigate communism in government and other areas of American life. Most of his charges proved to be unjustified, but his power was not broken until the Senate voted to censure him in 1954. He died in 1957.

Senator Brien McMahon of Connecticut drafted the Atomic Energy Act. He was the first chairman of a special Senate Committee on Atomic Energy, and his services for the peaceful use of atomic energy have been memorialized by a commemorative postage stamp.

Another political leader of Irish ancestry is Senator Eugene McCarthy of Minnesota. He stirred the Democratic National Convention in 1960 with his memorable nominating speech on behalf of Adlai Stevenson. In 1968, Senator McCarthy campaigned for the Democratic nomination for president. His outspoken idealism and opposition to the war in Vietnam made him a rallying point for many of the nation's college students. He won the New Hampshire primary but lost the nomination to Hubert Humphrey.

Brien McMahon, the late senator from Connecticut *(left),* was author of the Atomic Energy Act.

Senator Eugene McCarthy of Minnesota *(center).* He has served on the Senate Foreign Relations and Finance Committees.

Patrick V. McNamara, the late senator from Michigan *(right).*

Robert S. McNamara is another Irishman who has held high government positions. He is a Presbyterian, a holder of a Phi Beta Kappa key, and a graduate of Harvard School of Business. He was president of the Ford Motor Company when President-elect Kennedy appointed him Secretary of Defense. In 1968 McNamara became President of the World Bank.

Other Irishmen who are, or have been involved in politics are Kenneth Keating, Pat Brown, James Byrnes, Lawrence O'Brien and Daniel Moynihan. Kenneth Keating was one of the Senators from New York State until he was defeated by another Irishman, Robert Kennedy, in 1964. Pat Brown has served as governor of California. James Byrnes spent his life in many types of political activity. He was head of the Office of War Mobilization under President Franklin Roosevelt, Secretary of State and Supreme Court Justice under President Truman, and governor of the state of South Carolina.

Lawrence O'Brien, Postmaster General from 1965 to 1968, has organized campaigns for several Democratic political candidates. He helped organize President Kennedy's campaign for the Senate in 1952, and was the national organizer for the Kennedy-Johnson

Senator George Murphy of California *(left)*. He was a well-known movie personality before he entered politics.

Robert S. McNamara. He was appointed Secretary of Defense in the administration of President Kennedy and stayed on in the cabinet of President Johnson. He held this office longer than any other man, from 1961 until 1968.

Edmund G. "Pat" Brown, governor of California from 1959-1966 *(right).*

campaign of 1960. He was a top aide to Hubert Humphrey during the 1968 presidential campaign, during which he also served as Democratic National Chairman. Daniel Moynihan was appointed chief advisor to the Council on Urban Affairs, a cabinet-level post in the Nixon administration.

Several Americans of Irish ancestry have served on the United States Supreme Court. Among them are Justices Pierce Butler, who served from 1923 to 1939, Frank Murphy, who served from 1940 to 1949, and William J. Brennan, Jr., who was appointed to the court in 1956.

4. *The Kennedy Family*

The story of the Joseph P. Kennedy family perhaps best illustrates the success of the Irish-Americans in the political arena. Joseph Kennedy's grandfather, Patrick, landed in Boston in 1850 as a penniless immigrant who had fled the potato famine. In 1862 his son, also named Patrick, was born and he grew up to be a saloon-keeper and ward boss in the city of Boston. His son, Joseph, born in 1888, was a graduate of the Boston Latin School and Harvard University.

Joseph Kennedy became a bank president at the age of 26, and had made his first million by the time he was 35. His fortune was made by investments in motion pictures, real estate, stocks, and whiskey. The fortune which he controls today has been estimated at over 200 million dollars. He supported Franklin D. Roosevelt in 1932 and was appointed chairman of the Securities and Exchange Commission. In 1938 he became the first Catholic and the first Irishman to serve as American ambassador to the Court of St. James in London. It has been said that Joseph Kennedy wanted to succeed Franklin D. Roosevelt in the Presidency, but when that became improbable (because of a split with Roosevelt) he decided to bend his efforts toward making his son President.

Joseph, Jr. was his eldest son and the one to whom the father chose to devote his efforts. Joe, Jr. was a pilot in World War II who completed his required number of missions and was entitled to return home. He volunteered for one final mission which required that he and another man fly a B-17 bomber loaded with TNT explosives towards a German target. They were to parachute down in friendly territory when they were sure that the plane was on target. The plane was to go in on remote control. Something went wrong, and the plane blew up in mid-air. With the death of Joseph, Jr., John F., the next eldest son, became the one whom the father wanted to be President.

John F. Kennedy also served in World War II, but he was in the United States Navy as commander of a PT boat. The story of his adventures in the Pacific theater of war is well-known. A Japanese destroyer, the *Amagiri*, slashed the PT boat in two in 1943 at Blackett Straits near New Georgia. Two of the men were killed immediately and Kennedy performed feats of heroism getting the men who could not swim to land, obtaining food and water, and avoiding the hostile Japanese patrols. The men were finally rescued as friendly natives covered them with palm fronds and paddled their longboats past the Japanese sentries. Having survived this, JFK nearly died of malaria. He developed chronic back trouble which undoubtedly was caused by the destroyer ramming incident.

Upon returning home from the service, John Kennedy was persuaded by his father to enter politics and he won a seat in the

The Kennedy half-dollar, issued to memorialize our late 35th President.

House of Representatives for the 11th district of the state of Massachusetts. He served there for six years. In 1952 he defeated Henry Cabot Lodge for the Senate, but he failed in his bid for the Democratic Party Vice Presidential nomination in 1956. In November, 1960, however, he was elected as the 35th President of the United States.

Kennedy's election was a triumph for the American Irish in many respects. It wiped away some of the disappointment for the defeat of Al Smith in 1928. Since politics was the field in which many Irishmen had chosen to participate, the Presidency represented the highest political office attainable. Irishmen were justly

JOHN F. KENNEDY

proud of Kennedy's victory. He was the first Roman Catholic to be elected. The issue of a man's religion in regard to his qualification for the highest office in the land had been met head on. Kennedy was youthful and aggressive and he possessed the charm and wit which so many Irishmen had. His wife, Jacqueline, became known to millions of Americans and around the world. The White House became a family home where his daughter Caroline had her pony and his son John, Jr. romped about.

Kennedy was a fluent speaker, and the words of his inaugural address, "Ask not what your country can do for you, but what you can do for your country," were widely quoted. The Irish, a people who had produced many famous bards, singers, poets, actors and orators, had an excellent representative in John F. Kennedy.

It was probably a good thing for the Irish in America that he was just an average athlete and became a bookish man. The Irish had had many representatives in the field of sports, but John F. Kennedy demonstrated that there were things in life as important as making the team. The sports which he popularized were swimming, sailing, and touch football. His physical fitness program for the nation was for all age groups and both sexes. He was a tireless reader of good literature and set a good example for young people to develop their intellects as well as their bodies.

The Kennedy memorial postage stamp.

The Kennedy commemorative airmail stamp.

Edward M. Kennedy. He was elected Senator from Massachusetts in 1962. In January of 1969, he was elected majority whip in the Senate.

Robert F. Kennedy served as Attorney-General of the United States, and as Senator from New York.

The nation was horrified on November 22, 1963, to hear that their youthful President had been struck down by an assassin's bullet in the city of Dallas. Young and old, rich and poor, were grief stricken when it was announced that the President was dead. The nation mourned its loss, and the American Irish were deeply moved by the event.

In June of 1968, the nation again mourned a member of the Kennedy family when Senator Robert F. Kennedy, a candidate for the Democratic presidential nomination, was assassinated. The assassination occurred during the celebration following Kennedy's victory in the California primary. Prior to his election to the Senate in 1964, Kennedy had served as Attorney General in his brother's administration.

PART VIII

Conclusion

Americans no longer think of the Irish when they speak of the integration of the foreign-born into American life. Irishmen are still proud of their "Emerald Isle," but they are first and foremost Americans. England is no longer the cruel oppressor, since the future of Ireland is in Irish hands. The "Irish question" is no longer a burning issue and the reasons for a Sinn Fein movement have disappeared.

The Irish immigrants fought with courage against incredible hardships and earned the respect of their fellow American citizens. They endured discrimination and prejudice, and existed in lowly slums. The Irishman of the 19th century, however, no longer exists except in the imagination. "Paddy" has graduated to the ranks of the clerks, salesmen, businessmen, lawyers, and the clergy.

The wearing of green on St. Patrick's Day is no longer restricted solely to the Irish. Americans of many racial backgrounds wear a shamrock or a green ribbon in honor of Ireland's special day. The great St. Patrick's Day parade in New York City is an event enjoyed by millions of Americans. The dignitaries watching from the steps of St. Patrick's Cathedral often represent many racial backgrounds.

Irish music remains the favorite of millions on radio and television, and the sentiment it contains crosses national boundaries.

There are few groups, in fact, who have maintained their unique customs and characteristics, and yet have become so thoroughly identified with the meaning of America.

From 1820 to 1910, the total Irish immigration into the U.S. was 4,212,169. About 58 percent of this group live in the states of New York, Pennsylvania, Massachusetts, and Illinois. With the addition of the Irish in the states of Connecticut, New Jersey, Ohio, and California, the total would account for 75 percent of the American Irish. The Irish in this country have, in every census of the present century, exceeded the number of Irish living in Ireland. A research director for the American Council of Learned Societies estimated in 1928 that approximately 18 million Americans have Irish names.

Irish Immigration to the United States

1820-1829	51,617	1890-1899	405,890
1830-1839	170,472	1900-1909	344,940
1840-1849	656,118	1910-1919	166,445
1850-1859	1,029,476	1920-1929	206,737
1860-1869	427,419	1930-1939	35,773
1870-1879	422,264	1940-1945	1,898
1880-1889	674,151		

Today there are probably more than 20 million Americans who have some Irish ancestry. These have been so well assimilated that even the Friendly Sons of St. Patrick, though proud of their national origin and organizational history dating back to the Revolutionary War, think of themselves as "Americans of Irish Extraction." The recording secretary of this organization, Richard C. Murphy, recently stated, "We're not Irish who just happen to be living in America." The Friendly Sons of St. Patrick endeavored to prove that they are Americans first and foremost when they chose an American of English and Scottish extraction as their 1964 annual banquet speaker, President Lyndon B. Johnson.

The *Dictionary of American Biography* lists nearly 500 well-known Americans who were born in Ireland, and literally thousands of others who are of Irish descent. Orestes Brownson, a New England writer of the 19th century, proved to be somewhat prophetic when he said of the Irish: "Out of these narrow lanes, blind courts, dirty streets, damp cellars, and suffocating garrets, will come forth some of the noblest sons of our country, whom she will delight to own and honor." For many of the Irish this meant achieving middle class respectability. For others, this has meant achieving high goals in the arts or some profession. For some, such as John F. Kennedy, it has meant achieving the highest post which the nation can bestow on one of its citizens.

ACKNOWLEDGEMENTS

The illustrations are reproduced through the courtesy of: pp. 6, 8, 9, 10, 13, 15, 17, 19, 22, 27, 32, 34, 35, 47 (top), 48 (top center, bottom left, bottom center), 55 (left), 56 (bottom), 65, Independent Pictures; pp. 12, 29, 31 (left and right), 44, 47 (bottom), 49, 54, Library of Congress; p. 21, Northern Pacific Railroad; p. 38, Standard Oil; p. 40, Pinkerton's, Inc. Archives; p. 41, AFL-CIO; p. 45 (left), Charles Scribner's Sons; p. 45 (center), Random House, Inc.; p. 45 (right), Vanguard Press; p. 48 (top left, bottom right), TV Times; p. 48 (top right), Station WCCO, Minneapolis; p. 50, 620 Club, Minneapolis; p. 51, National Baseball Hall of Fame; p. 52 (left), Cleveland Browns; p. 52 (right), Wheaties Sports Foundation; p. 53, Minnesota Historical Society; p. 55 (right), Roosevelt University; pp. 56 (top left and right), 70 (center), United States Army; p. 58, Farrar, Straus, Giroux, Inc.; p. 63, Office of the Mayor; p. 66, Office of the Representative; p. 67, The Coca-Cola Export Corporation; pp. 69 (left), 74, Post Office Department, Division of Philately; pp. 69 (center), 73, Democratic-Farmer-Labor Party; pp. 69 (right), 70 (left), 75 (left and right), Office of the Senator; p. 70 (right), Office of the Governor; p. 72, The Smithsonian Institution, Division of Numismatics.

ABOUT THE AUTHOR

JAMES E. JOHNSON was born in Johnson City, New York. After service in the Navy, he obtained his Bachelor of Arts Degree from the Triple Cities College of Syracuse University and his Master of Arts Degree from the University of Buffalo. In 1959, Syracuse University granted him a Doctor of Philosophy Degree in history. He is a member of the American Historical Association, the Organization of American Historians, and Phi Gamma Mu, the National Social Science Honor Society. Dr. Johnson taught United States history at Youngstown University and is now Professor of History at Bethel College, St. Paul, Minnesota.

The IN AMERICA *Series*

We specialize in publishing quality books for
young people. For a complete list please write:

LERNER PUBLICATIONS COMPANY
241 First Avenue North, Minneapolis, Minnesota 55401